GUIDE TO THE PINCHOT TRAIL SYSTEM

SECOND EDITION

BEN CRAMER

CATAMOUNT
PRESS

an imprint of Sunbury Press, Inc.
Mechanicsburg, PA USA

CATAMOUNT
PRESS

an imprint of Sunbury Press, Inc.
Mechanicsburg, PA USA

For information about special discounts for bulk purchases, please contact Sunbury Press Orders Dept. at (855) 338-8359 or orders@sunburypress.com.

To request one of our authors for speaking engagements or book signings, please contact Sunbury Press Publicity Dept. at publicity@sunburypress.com.

FIRST CATAMOUNT PRESS EDITION: October 2025

Set in Adobe Garamond | Interior design by Crystal Devine | Cover by Lawrence Knorr | Edited by Debra Reynolds. All photos by the author.

Publisher's Cataloging-in-Publication Data
Names: Cramer, Ben, author.
Title: Guide to the Pinchot Trail System / Ben Cramer.
Description: First trade paperback edition. | Mechanicsburg, PA : Catamount Press, 2025.
Summary: A point-by-point guide to the Pinchot Trail System, a 22-mile double loop that travels through Pinchot State Forest in Lackawanna County, Pennsylvania.
Identifiers: ISBN : 979-8-88819-352-5 (softcover).
Subjects: SPORTS & RECREATION / Hiking | TRAVEL / Northeast / Middle Atlantic (NJ, NJ, PA) | NATURE / Regional.

Designed in the USA
0 1 1 2 3 5 8 13 21 34 55

For the Love of Books!

Cover: Choke Creek Falls, reached via the south section of the Pinchot Trail System.

TABLE OF CONTENTS

AUTHOR'S NOTE

This trail guide accurately reflects measurements and observations that were made along the Pinchot Trail System during an inspection by the author in Spring 2024. Original measurements taken for the previous edition of this guidebook in 2019 have been re-checked for accuracy. All efforts have been made to ensure accuracy in descriptions of the features and logistics of the trail and the distances involved. However, conditions in the natural world are constantly changing. Fallen trees, flash floods, forestry practices, human developments, and myriad other phenomena often necessitate the rerouting of hiking trails and can damage infrastructure such as footbridges. Changes in the route or condition of the trail may be completed by the Pennsylvania Department of Conservation and Natural Resources, Keystone Trails Association, or other volunteers after this guide is published.

All persons using this guide do so at their own risk, and this guide should not be used without adequate maps and other common sense precautions, which should be practiced by all outdoorspersons. The author, publisher, and all trail workers/volunteers disclaim any and all liability for trail conditions, hazards, incidents encountered by hikers, and inaccuracies in this guide that may be the result of future developments. Also, the reader should follow this guide's recommendations for water sources and camping locations at their own risk. Please contact the author about any changes encountered along the trail that should be included in future editions of this guide.

ACKNOWLEDGMENTS

The joy of hiking in Pennsylvania would not be possible without the contributions of volunteer trail builders, maintainers, and observers. Hikers and backpackers may not even notice the valuable work of these volunteers, but they would surely notice if all that hard work was no longer being performed. Thanks to all the trail club volunteers and state forest employees in Pennsylvania who make our trails so enjoyable.

In particular for the trails discussed in this guide, I would like to enthusiastically thank forestry workers Carl Sarti, Westley Stout, and Pete Loiacono, who were very friendly and helpful when I unexpectedly ran into them at a work location during my June 2024 inspection of the Pinchot Trail System. Thanks also to forester Tim Latz for providing information on trail developments during a scratchy cellular call in the deep wilderness.

The previous edition of this guide was greatly enhanced by the help received from Matthew Crosbie, Maggie McNamara, and Pinchot State Forest staff. Thanks also to Jeff Mitchell and Ed Lawrence of Keystone Trails Association for providing information on trail improvement projects. And finally, special thanks to Brook Lenker of Keystone Trails Association for providing a connection with Sunbury Press, where Lawrence Knorr and his team have been instrumental in getting this book into your hands.

Ben Cramer, June 2025

ABOUT THE PINCHOT TRAIL SYSTEM

INTRODUCTION

The Pinchot (pronounced "Pin-Cho") Trail System is a 22.21-mile-long loop in the Thornhurst Tract of Pinchot State Forest in the Pocono region of northeastern Pennsylvania. The loop is nestled in the extreme southern tip of Lackawanna County, about ten miles as the crow flies from Wilkes-Barre.

The trail was named after a hero of Pennsylvania conservationism, Gifford Pinchot (1865–1946). Originally from Connecticut but with a family estate in Milford, Pike County, Pinchot was an early pioneer of forestry management practices, and from 1905 to 1910 served as the first chief of the United States Forest Service. In that position Pinchot often made the news for his ideological differences with President Theodore Roosevelt; Pinchot favored scientific analysis and structured management of forest resource usage (influencing what is now known as the "Wise Use" school of conservationism) while Roosevelt favored the preservation of wilderness areas for their aesthetic value. The longtime friends eventually fell out and Pinchot was fired from the Forest Service. He was later Governor of Pennsylvania twice and his influence continues to be felt throughout Pennsylvania politics and forestry management practices.

The forest tract through which the Pinchot Trail travels was known as Lackawanna State Forest until 2015, when various state-owned land parcels were expanded and consolidated. The reorganized tract was renamed Pinchot State Forest, with its headquarters at Lackawanna State Park north of Scranton.

The Pinchot Trail System is indeed a "system" that was formed from segments of several previously existing trails. In the 1970s, a local Sierra Club volunteer and retired truck driver named Frank Gantz constructed a large loop hike in the former Lackawanna State Forest by piecing together older trail segments and building some new connectors. Since then, the system has been rerouted and expanded several times under the management of Keystone Trails Association. The most recent such project was in 2018, when significant new trail segments were built to replace a long walk along Tannery Road. In 2024, the Pinchot Trail was adopted by the Susquehanna Trailers Hiking Club of Wilkes-Barre, with volunteers from that club maintaining the trail regularly.

BLAZES AND TRAIL SIGNS

The Pinchot Trail System loop is marked with continuous orange blazes. While hiking around the loop, you will see signs with other trail names, such as the Stone Lookout Trail, Sunday Trail, Painter Creek Trail, and several others. These are the older trails that were subsumed into the Pinchot loop. This results in the odd situation in which you are consciously following a resource promoted by the state as the "Pinchot Trail System" while seeing very few trail signs with that name.

It has been common in Pennsylvania hiking history for long loops to be formed out of segments of older trails that were shorter and unidirectional as backpacking loops became more popular over time. In such cases, a new loop was given a distinct name of its own while the previous trail names and signs were retained for their historic interest. (The 83-mile-long Susquehannock Trail System in Potter County is Pennsylvania's prime example of this trail-naming process.)

While the older trail names are indeed of historic interest, I have never been a fan of this technique, because it can cause unnecessary confusion, especially for novice hikers who may have endeavored to follow a continuous trail with a title like "Pinchot Trail System" but keep seeing signs with different names. At the time of writing, such trail signs with older names are still present on the Pinchot Trail System.

The managers of Pinchot State Forest have discussed ways to address this confusion at some future date, possibly by adding new signs that say "Pinchot Trail System" or "PTS" continuously. This has not yet happened as of the time of writing, so the older names are described in this guide to denote crucial turns and junctions.

THE POCONO LANDSCAPE

Most of the Pinchot Trail System traverses a high-plateau landscape that is typical of the Pocono region. The average elevation of the trail is around 1,900 feet, and the plateau-top areas offer generally easy hiking. However, there are noticeable descents into and climbs back out of the valleys of Painter Creek on the north section of the loop and Choke Creek on the south section.

The highest point in the system is at about 2,220 feet on top of a hill south of Painter Creek, and the lowest points are along Sand Creek and then Choke Creek in the southeastern portion of the loop, each at about 1,670 feet. If you hike the loop clockwise as described in this guide, your total elevation gain will be a little more than 2,000 feet, which is quite manageable over the course of 22 miles.

It is important to note that the Pocono region is infamously wet and muddy. The reason the area has a lot of natural lakes, especially in flat plateau-top areas, is because of a lumpy landscape and a vast layer of hard underlying rock that invites the accumulation of water in the form of puddles big and small. In short, the land does not soak up water very well, and it tends to sit around. Thus, many hikers have learned that the flatter areas of the Pinchot Trail System are prone to not just mud for much of the year, but even wide areas of standing water during wet periods.

Do not let this spook you because the trail still offers a rewarding hiking experience at all times. Just be prepared. Anyone hiking this trail is advised to prepare for mud at any time of the year and to bring rugged footwear and extra socks if it has been raining recently. The good news is that, unlike most of Pennsylvania's long-distance backpacking trails, the Pinchot Trail System is largely (but not entirely) free of jagged rocks underfoot.

PLANTS AND WILDLIFE

While hiking the Pinchot Trail System, you will be treated to the flora and fauna that are unique to the Pocono region. Wildflower lovers are in for a particular treat. In the 1990s, a local enthusiast named Jane

A flowering bush, seen in the springtime along the north section
of the Pinchot Trail System.

Frye, with some help from trail founder Frank Gantz and District Forester Anthony Santoli, inventoried the plant life to be found in this area
of Pinchot State Forest (then known as Lackawanna State Forest). Frye
located 78 different species of flowering plants, including several that are
rare or unknown elsewhere in the northeastern United States.

Depending on the season, you are likely to see several different types
of huckleberries, blueberries, and dewberries; trailing arbutuses, trilliums,
and violets; and even wild oats and sarsaparilla. The Pocono region also
hosts several unique plant species that are unlikely to be found elsewhere
in Pennsylvania, such as Venus flytraps and witch hazel.

In addition to common Pennsylvania trees like oak, beech, and hem-
lock, you will also see some fairly uncommon species including yellow
birch and spruce, which in this area are quite close to the limits of their
natural ranges. Only a few examples of plants and trees are mentioned
here, but the interested naturalist can find much more information
(including an excellent illustrated brochure) from the staffs at Pinchot
State Forest and the nearby state parks.

Just as it does for unique plant life, the Pocono region hosts many
unique animal species due to its geography and geology. I have witnessed
many uncommon frog and salamander species in the area. And while

I am not an expert bird watcher, I certainly noticed a lot of unfamiliar songbirds and a variety of hawks in the area. Bird-watching enthusiasts are highly encouraged to visit the Pinchot Trail System for a taste of the region's diverse avian life.

The wildlife in the region includes plenty of the animals that are found most often in other wild areas of Pennsylvania, such as deer, groundhogs, and rabbits. Bears and rattlesnakes are also prevalent in the region; I have seen neither of these on the Pinchot Trail but have seen specimens of both elsewhere in the Poconos, including along the Thunder Swamp Trail, another long-distance loop in Pike County about 30 miles to the east.

Predators should not be a serious concern for hikers if one exercises common sense. Black bears tend to flee from humans long before they are seen, thanks to their remarkable sense of smell. A hiker should consider it great luck to even see one. Bears should not be provoked and definitely should not be fed, which increases the chances of their behavior changing abruptly from docile to aggressive.

There is a chance of bears harassing untended campsites, though this should not be a serious concern for backpackers who take the necessary precautions. Porcupines and coyotes are also common in the area, and these scavengers have been known to disturb untended campsites. However, both of these animals are quite skittish and are highly unlikely to confront humans directly.

The only truly dangerous animal in this area is the eastern timber rattlesnake. This snake prefers open areas for sunning and rocky outcrops for building dens. This species is venomous, but its bites are typically not fatal to healthy humans, with only a medium-strength temporary illness resulting for most people. (However, some people are highly allergic to the venom, leading to a more serious illness, and are probably unaware of their allergy until it is too late. Also, extra vigilance should be exercised for one's smaller hiking companions, such as dogs and young children.)

If bitten by a rattlesnake along the trail, do not panic. Return to your car quickly but in a levelheaded manner and seek medical attention as soon as possible. Contrary to popular opinion, rattlesnakes rarely attack humans—but rather defend themselves when provoked. In a telling reflection of human nature, upward of 80% of snakebite victims anywhere in the world are bitten on their hands and arms, after stupidly trying to pick up the snake. In the rare event that you encounter an eastern timber rattlesnake, retreat sensibly, leave it alone, and consider yourself lucky to have seen this unique creature in its natural habitat.

A different problem arises from insects. Mosquitoes and similar pests are ubiquitous in the region, as are ticks. Lyme Disease has been reported in the area, and encounters with ticks (only a few of which actually carry the disease) are on the rise. High-quality insect repellent is crucial on Pennsylvania hiking trails during all seasons except the deepest parts of winter.

There is one additional critter that deserves an honorable mention here. Beavers are very common in the region, and their vigorous landscaping endeavors are often quite visible along the Pinchot Trail. During various visits over the years, I have observed the trail disappearing, as the critters dammed nearby streams for their own purposes. At the time of your visit, those particular beaver dams may no longer exist, but it is equally likely that new ones will have been built. This may require sloshing through water during your hike or taking difficult detours through the nearby trees. Note that it is the current policy of Pinchot State Forest to let nature take its course, and beaver dams are not typically removed unless they pose significant risk to human visitors.

A NOTE ON HUNTING

The plentiful wildlife in this area attracts a thriving hunting industry, and hikers must exercise caution in the presence of hunters. The author of this guide and the associated trail maintainers and Commonwealth personnel disavow all responsibility for the danger in which hikers may place themselves when hunters are present. Avoid hiking in state forest areas during the big game hunting seasons in the fall and early winter. If necessary, inquire with State Forest personnel beforehand to learn which areas of the forest attract the most hunters. The Pennsylvania Game Commission also manages hunting seasons for many types of small game throughout the rest of the year, though these seasons present little risk for the hiker. Nevertheless, anyone hiking in areas known to be frequented by hunters is strongly advised to wear at least one prominent piece of "safety orange" clothing for visibility.

ACCESS AND LOGISTICS

BACKPACKING TRIPS AND DAY HIKES

The Pinchot Trail System is laid out as a long loop that (with some imagination) is roughly bean-shaped, wide at its top and bottom and pinched in the middle. The paved Bear Lake Road passes through the narrow portion near the center of the loop, dividing the system into two segments that have traditionally been called the South Section and North Section. As described in this guide, the total length of the loop (South and North Sections combined) is 22.21 miles. This distance could be covered in a very long day hike by expert hikers. Beginners or those wishing for a more relaxed pace can easily complete the entire loop as a two-day/one-night backpacking trip.

The trail's layout, with Bear Lake Road passing near its middle, also enables robust day hikes on each of the sections to either side of that road. The point-by-point description of the trail system in this guidebook uses a parking lot at the corner of Bear Lake Road and Tannery Road at its starting point, and this parking lot also divides the overall trail into southern and northern sub-loops.

To hike only the South Section of the Pinchot Trail System, start at the trailhead parking lot and follow this guidebook from points 0.00 to 12.86, then walk 0.43 miles on Bear Lake Road back to the parking lot, for a total distance of 13.29 miles. To hike only the North Section, start with the 0.43 miles on Bear Lake Road, then follow this guidebook from points 12.86 to 22.21, for a total distance of 9.78 miles.

Both of those possibilities are described in the point-by-point trail description later in this book. The area's yellow-blazed side trails can also be used to form shorter loop hikes. Some such possibilities are mentioned in the trail description, and hikers who are good at reading maps and estimating distances will be able to envision several other day hiking options.

In addition to short loop hikes where they can be arranged, the author of this book strongly recommends day hikes of the out-and-back variety. Start at one of the more accessible parking spots, follow the trail for a certain distance, then turn around and return to your car. Not only can you tell your friends that you have completed that section of the trail twice, but this is a useful technique for piecing together a series of day hikes into a complete transit of a long-distance trail. Besides, hikers are often surprised by how much scenery they can miss by following a trail in only one direction. Just note that the trail descriptions in this book are one-way so if you are going in the opposite direction, left turns become right turns, uphill becomes downhill, and the like.

MEASURING AND MAPPING TECHNIQUE

Your present author personally measured and mapped the Pinchot Trail System specifically for the first edition of this book in 2019. I used a Garmin Oregon 550 handheld GPS device and carefully corrected the resulting data to achieve maps and tables of measurements that were as close to reality as possible. In June 2024 I completed the trail again and made notes of a few minor changes that have been included in this new edition of the guidebook

The final measurement for the Pinchot Trail System achieved via this method is 22.21 miles (35.77 kilometers). Since its founding in the 1970s, the trail has been relocated and expanded many times, and almost all of the trail improvement projects over the years significantly altered its length. This has caused some historical uncertainty about the trail's total hiking distance. I have seen descriptions of the Pinchot Trail System in various books, magazines, and websites from various time periods describing it as anywhere from 21 to 26 miles long. The estimates at the higher end of that range are something of a mystery; the writers may have included road walking or connector trails to form sub-loops.

In any case, please accept the figures in this book as "official" until the next volunteer comes along to measure the trail again. Admittedly, the accuracy of on-the-ground distance measurements via GPS has not yet been fully acknowledged by trail maintainers and veteran hikers, though most have accepted the accuracy of GPS mapping. A measuring wheel, which uses an odometer to measure feet or meters as the hiker pushes it along the trail, is remarkably accurate, even among multiple people who measure the same trail and compare their numbers. I once preferred to use such a device myself, but my most recent model broke in the middle of measurements for one of my previous guidebooks, and due to time pressures I was unable to replace it and instead learned how to carefully manage the data collected by my GPS device.

The maps included in this guide were created from the author's GPS data that was downloaded into professional mapping software. In the final pages of this book you will find small maps, plus a QR code and website address that can be used to access a more detailed online map, which was also created from the author's GPS data.

In addition, there is an excellent public use map denoting the Pinchot Trail System and several affiliated side trails, published by Pinchot State Forest. The most recent version of this map (at the time of writing) was published in 2019.

BLAZES AND TRAIL CHARACTERISTICS

As an official Pennsylvania State Forest hiking trail, the Pinchot Trail System is marked with orange blazes. Affiliated side trails are marked with yellow blazes. Note that these color designations have changed several times over the years while some former routes of the Pinchot Trail were decommissioned and reclassified as side trails. Therefore, older maps may cause some confusion as to trail routes and blaze colors.

Thanks to the efforts of Commonwealth personnel and volunteer trail maintainers, the blazes are generally plentiful and easy to follow, except for a few problematic areas that are described in this guide. Sharp turns are usually denoted by double blazes and occasionally arrows. The rectangular blazes are typically painted on trees alongside the trail and are usually visible from a comfortable distance. In some treeless spots, poles have been secured in the ground to bear the blazes. Blazes are also occasionally on rocks underfoot.

ACCESS POINTS AND PARKING

Despite its proximity to the Scranton/Wilkes-Barre metropolitan area, reaching the Pinchot Trail System by road is a rather involved process. The paved Bear Lake Road bisects the trail, and this road connects to plenty of other paved roads in the area, but the drive to the trailhead is surprisingly lengthy.

This guidebook uses an official State Forest parking lot at the corner of Bear Lake Road and Tannery Road as its recommended starting point. This spot is in southern Lackawanna County, near a border with Luzerne County to the east of Wilkes-Barre.

GPS LOCATION: N41° 12.934' W75° 38.534'

Perhaps the easiest way to reach this parking lot is from PA 115. From the Wilkes-Barre area, follow PA 115 for 9.2 miles south of I-81 (or 4.9 miles south of I-476). You can also follow PA 115 for 11.0 miles north from I-80 near Blakeslee. In either case, reach an intersection with a traffic light at Meadow Run Road. Turn northeast onto this road and follow it for 3.8 miles until it ends at Thornhurst Road near a dam and an artificial lake. Turn right (east) on Thornhurst Road, which later changes its name to Bear Lake Road, and drive for 1.9 miles to the corner of Tannery Road, where you will find the gravel parking lot that serves as the Pinchot trailhead.

OTHER OPTIONS FOR REACHING THE MAIN TRAILHEAD

From the Scranton area, use PA 315 to Dupont. From that borough's downtown, take Bear Creek Road to the southeast, soon passing both I-81 and I-476. Continue southeast, then south, as the name changes to Suscon Road then Thornhurst Road. The paved road then curves broadly to the east and becomes Bear Lake Road. Reach the parking lot at the corner of Tannery Road, 11.2 miles from Dupont.

From the east, use I-380 to the exit for PA 435 and PA 507. Travel north on PA 435 for 1.5 miles, then turn southwest on Clifton Beach Road. Follow this road for 7.2 miles; along the way it changes its name to Buck River Road. Then turn northwest on Bear Lake Road and follow it for 4.8 miles to the parking lot at the corner of Tannery Road.

OTHER PARKING AREAS

There is a larger Pinchot Trail parking area on Bear Lake Road, 0.6 miles east of the trailhead parking lot described above. This lot might be more convenient for overnight parking and is definitely bigger, but it is not situated on the South Section of the Pinchot Trail System and therefore is not useful for hikers doing only that section. This lot is recommended for hikers doing the North Section or the entire loop, and is at the trail's 21.56 mile point.

GPS LOCATION: N41° 13.161' W75° 37.883'

There is an additional parking area on Pittston Road just north of Bear Lake Road. Use the latter road, 1.0 miles east of the trailhead at the corner of Tannery Road. Turn north on the unpaved Pittston Road and proceed 0.3 miles to a gravel lot on the right that serves several different hiking and equestrian trails. The Pinchot Trail follows Pittston Road for a while in this area; the lot is at the trail's 20.54 mile point.

GPS LOCATION: N41° 13.373' W75° 37.320'

There is another parking area on Tannery Road, which is not on the main Pinchot Trail System but allows access via a side trail. From the corner of Bear Lake Road and Tannery Road as described above, follow the unpaved Tannery Road south then east for a total of 1.9 miles. There are a couple of different gravel parking areas near the north end of a yellow-blazed nature trail. Follow that trail southwest for 0.24 miles and reach the Pinchot Trail at its 10.65 mile point. Note that Tannery Road is gated and may not be accessible late at night or during the winter.

GPS LOCATION: N41° 12.023' W75° 37.890'

The Pinchot Trail System crosses several other unpaved roads along its length. Experienced hikers will know that such roads might have wide spots near a trail crossing where one or two cars can park. Some such possibilities are described in this guide at the applicable crossing points. However, for any road crossing that does not have a developed parking lot as described above, you would be using these access points at your own risk.

CAMPING

Pinchot State Forest offers robust options for casual campers and experienced backpackers. In many areas along the Pinchot Trail system, you will be undisturbed during your nighttime sojourn, but other areas are very popular with overnighters, maybe too much so, especially along Choke Creek. That and some other areas along the trail are easily reached by car and might be inhabited by weekenders with a different attitude than hikers.

On the good side, the relatively short length and usually benign landscapes of the Pinchot Trail System make it a great resource for beginning backpackers. This is a good place to practice your overnight skills and assess your ability to carry the heavy pack needed for tougher projects in the future. Consider taking the opportunity to park at a trailhead and walk a relatively short distance to a camping spot.

In Pennsylvania State Forest terminology, backcountry camping comes in two flavors: "car camping" (where you can park directly at a campsite) and "primitive camping" (on foot with a backpack). The latter is permitted anywhere in State Forest lands, with some restrictions as listed below.

Primitive camping spots that backpackers would consider "favorable" (a flat spot with a nearby stream and shady trees overhead) are quite common along the Pinchot Trail System, and there are also many pleasant but dry high-altitude spots if you prefer to camp under the stars.

In Pinchot State Forest, statewide camping rules apply. The Pennsylvania Department of Conservation and Natural Resources maintains rules and regulations for primitive camping on State Forest lands. The Commonwealth utilizes camping permits, which are mostly used for recordkeeping and safety purposes, and are free of charge at the time of this writing. Also at the time of writing, primitive backpackers are not required to apply for a camping permit except if any of the following conditions apply:

- An emergency point of contact is desired.
- You plan to stay at the same site for more than one night.

- A campfire is planned during the spring or fall fire seasons.
- You are "group camping" (more than 10 people).

This process is designed to control the damage that could result from large numbers of campers in sensitive areas. Note that camping permits are not issued to persons under 18. To apply for a camping permit, visit the DCNR website at www.dcnr.pa.gov. The site will direct you to navigate to the page for the applicable state forest district office where you will then find the necessary contact information and instructions.

IMPORTANT PRIMITIVE CAMPING RULES

DCNR maintains many rules for primitive camping in the state forests. Some of these will seem like common sense to experienced outdoorspersons, but others are unique to Pennsylvania conditions. For the most up-to-date rules, see the official state document "Primitive Camping in State Forests and Parks" which can also be found at the DCNR website.

Backpackers in Pennsylvania should observe the following important rules, among others:

- Carry out all trash. Repeat: ALL trash.
- Choose a spot that does not require the clearing of vegetation.
- Stay at least 100 feet away from any flowing stream or open water source.
- Do not wash clothes, dishes, or campsite equipment directly in a stream or spring. Collect water in a container and do your washing away from the source, then dispose of the wastewater at least 200 feet from the source.
- Whenever possible, camp at least 25 feet from the trail and preferably out of sight of the trail.
- Dispose of human waste by burying it in a hole at least 6 inches deep. Bring a camp trowel or small shovel for this purpose. Disposal sites should be at least 200 feet from water sources.
- Do not build a campfire during the dry seasons of spring and fall or during other periods of abnormally high fire danger. At other times, small campfires are permitted. At previously unused campsites, construct a fire ring with nearby rocks to prevent the flames from spreading, and scatter the ring before leaving the site.

- Do not chop down live trees for firewood. Only use downed and dead wood near your campsite. Power saws are not permitted except with prior permission from the relevant state forest office.

Also, though it is not a state forest rule, beware of camping in or near the many copses of giant rhododendron and mountain laurel along the Pinchot Trail System. These plants are flammable and may also provide cover for disagreeable animals.

CAMPING LOCATIONS MENTIONED IN THIS GUIDE

The author has made an effort to point out potential primitive camping spots along the trail, with selections being made for variety and the potential for pleasant backpacking experiences. However, not all of these sites may completely comply with the above rules. Some areas within larger "sites" listed in this guide may not be 100 feet from a water source or 25 feet from the trail. The hiker will also notice many existing campsites created by previous backpackers, which may not comply with either of those strictures. The mention of such sites in this guide should not be considered an endorsement of the possibly illegal activities of previous backpackers.

Many of the possible campsites mentioned in this guide are near streams and springs, and to follow the state forest rules you would have to find a spot along the edge of such an area that is sufficiently removed from the water. All backpackers are strongly advised to follow the DCNR's primitive camping rules, which will ensure that future backpackers will not be deprived of the opportunity. Those using this guide will camp at the described spots at their own risk.

WATER

In this age of acid rain and bacterial pathogens, all water sources encountered in the wild should be viewed with suspicion. Most of the Pocono region has plentiful streams and springs, and the natural water supply in the highland areas is fairly clean compared to that in nearby valley areas, notwithstanding a few exceptions as noted in this guide.

Giardia, a waterborne bacterium that causes the gastro-intestinal illness *giardiasis*, has been found in mountain streams throughout Pennsylvania. While experienced outdoorspersons might be comfortable drinking wild water, no hiking guide (including this one) will recommend doing so, and such actions will be taken at your own risk.

Water found along the trail should be treated with iodine capsules or submicron filters, which can be found at sports stores and outfitters. This is the recommended strategy for backpackers. The old-school method of purifying water by boiling it at a campfire is a tedious chore that is usually not worth the effort, even when boiling is actually achieved via a small wood fire. Day hikers should have little difficulty merely packing up the water they will need at home before embarking on their day trips.

WATER SOURCES LISTED IN THIS GUIDE

As of 2024, the present author has completed the trails described in this guide multiple times during various seasons of the year and has made an effort in this guide to describe the quality and seasonality of the water sources encountered along the trails. However, the user of this guide will consume any water found along the trail at their own risk. As a general rule, water found in muddy spots, seep springs, and backwaters along the sides of flowing streams should be avoided. Also, water from larger creeks should be avoided because wide waterways, by definition, have collected water from many tributaries and low-lying areas, increasing the chances of pollution. Also avoid taking water from streams that sport beaver dams, which alter natural filtration patterns.

This guide describes the suspected water quality (in the experienced hiker's estimation) of the many springs and small streams encountered along the trails discussed. These readings were *not* determined scientifically, should *not* be taken as any type of recommendation to drink the water, and should be considered as loose guidelines only. Water sources listed here as "poor" or "not suitable" should be avoided under all circumstances. Sources described as "questionable" could possibly be consumed by the desperate or hikers with high-quality filters, though such actions should be unnecessary in this region because better sources are almost always available nearby. A fair number of water sources are described as "acceptable," "good," or "excellent" in this guide. Water from these sources can be consumed by any hiker with store-bought filtering equipment.

A final note on water sources described in this guide: If you visit the trails during an especially dry period, beware that the flow and quality of springs and streams as described in this guide may be reduced. In fact, some may not even be flowing by the time you reach them. Wherever possible, efforts have been made to determine the quality of water sources during various seasons.

GUIDE TO THE PINCHOT TRAIL SYSTEM

This guide describes the Pinchot Trail System as starting at the trail-head parking lot at the corner of Bear Lake Road and Tannery Road, as explained in the "Access and Logistics" chapter above. The point-by-point trail description is then given in the clockwise direction, first heading south from the trailhead.

Describing the trail in this fashion was an arbitrary decision by the author; descriptions of the trail in other publications might be in the opposite direction. You are free to hike in any direction you want.

The point-by-point description describes the Pinchot Trail System loop in its entirety, with a total distance of 22.21 miles (35.77 kilometers). For planning purposes, the description is divided into a South Section and North Section relative to Bear Lake Road.

These two distinct sections could be used to form shorter sub-loops; in each case you would walk 0.43 miles on Bear Lake Road. In this fashion, the South Section can be used to form a sub-loop of 13.29 miles, and the North Section can be used to form a sub-loop of 9.78 miles.

SOUTH SECTION

MI	KM	DESCRIPTION
0.00	0.00	Start from the parking lot at the corner of Bear Lake Road and Tannery Road. To follow either the entire Pinchot Trail System or only the south loop, follow the orange blazes southbound past the "Head On Parking" sign. The trail meanders through evergreens and then proceeds to an open hardwood forest.
		(If you wish to follow the north loop only, walk west on Bear Lake Road for 0.43 mi [0.69 km] to the point where the other segment of the Pinchot Trail crosses

MI	KM	DESCRIPTION
(cont.)		the road, just before the county line. Turn right onto a footpath at a signpost. Then follow this guidebook from its 12.86 mi point.)
0.27	0.44	Turn left at a trail junction. (To the right is an old version of the Pinchot Trail that was decommissioned to get the hiker off Tannery Road.) After your left turn, proceed through a jungle of mountain laurel and giant rhododendron.
0.39	0.63	Turn right abruptly at a junction with an overgrown side trail.
0.71	1.14	Emerge from a particularly dense rhododendron jungle and rise briefly to higher ground. Note the abrupt change from rhododendron to mountain laurel as the dominant shrub.
0.82	1.32	Enter a large brushy meadow where you will see lots of wildflowers in the spring.

Just south of Bear Lake Road, the Pinchot Trail strides across this meadow.

MI	KM	DESCRIPTION
0.98	1.58	After the meadow, enter a young forest. The trail curves broadly to the left (northeast).
1.25	2.01	Pass through a wet, swampy area caused by several seep springs and lack of drainage. Next, join what appears to be an old road grade. There are some more soggy areas ahead.
1.44	2.31	Pass a signpost denoting the McClintock's Gate Trail and Stone Lookout Trail and continue ahead. These pre-existing trails were incorporated into the Pinchot Trail System.
		Note: As described earlier in this book, the old signs with the pre-existing trail names could possibly be removed in the future, but as of the time of writing they remain in place. This will be relevant for many junctions described below.
1.61	2.60	Begin a steep but relatively brief climb up a ridgeline. The trail then levels off in a high meadow.
1.72	2.77	Enter a large gravel area. At the far side, avoid the incoming access road and bear left onto a footpath.
1.81	2.91	Pass through another meadow. This is an intriguing but dry campsite. Bear right at a large pile of loose rocks, which constitutes the remains of a stone lookout tower. The trail then descends briefly through a rocky area.
		A 15-foot stone tower was first built at this spot in 1890 as a monument to a local man who had died in a boating accident. The monument was modified in 1913 for use as a fire lookout. The stone tower soon became obsolete as much taller wooden towers were developed, while the fire-spotting task is now performed with aircraft.
1.92	3.10	Turn left on a forestry road and follow it for the next 0.45 mi (0.72 km). After the first big curve in the road, the gravel ends, and you continue ahead as the road changes to a grassy lane.

MI	KM	DESCRIPTION
2.37	3.82	Turn right at a junction of grassy woods roads. Note the sign for the Stone Lookout Trail. Stay on this second road for the next 0.24 mi (0.38 km).
2.49	4.01	Continue straight ahead at another junction. (The lane to the left is marked as the Golf Course Trail.)
2.61	4.20	Just before a muddy pit in the road, watch for a sign-post denoting the Sunday Trail and turn abruptly left onto a footpath. Watch for this turn carefully.
2.85	4.59	The trail bears right into a low rocky area, which tends to get flooded during wet periods.
2.99	4.82	Turn right at a lumpy spot (possibly the site of old railroad construction), then descend into another low area that may also be flooded during high water periods. There are a few more wet areas ahead where small streams sometimes commandeer the trail.
3.32	5.35	Cross the intersection of Tannery Road and Fireline Road at an angle and join the former Birch Still Trail. There is no easy parking within sight of this road crossing.
3.78	6.09	Sand Spring Creek appears to the left of the trail. This is the first robust water source of the hike, but its quality is questionable in this area.
4.01	6.46	The trail is on relatively high ground with Sand Spring Creek still to the left. The low area between the trail and creek offers some possible camping spots, though this is generally a soggy area.
4.17	6.71	Skirt the edge of a meadow; note the old gas pipes.
4.35	7.01	Jog left briefly on Phelps Road and continue into the woods. There is a possible parking spot down the road to the left.
4.50	7.25	Hop across a tributary of Sand Spring Creek; acceptable water quality. This crossing will be tricky during high water periods.

MI	KM	DESCRIPTION
4.84	7.79	Cross a grassy lane and continue straight ahead. Next, pass through a plantation of very tall red pines.
5.28	8.49	Cross a wide but overgrown woods road and continue ahead.
5.43	8.75	Jog right briefly on Phelps Road (your second encounter with this road), then turn back into the woods. There is possible parking for one or two cars at wide spots in the road here.
5.51	8.88	Watch carefully for an abrupt left turn at a great campsite. The trail heads south, parallel to Butler Run. If you miss this turn, you will find yourself on the yellow-blazed Butler Run Trail, a former route of the Pinchot Trail. In 2018, the Pinchot Trail was rerouted here, turning left to reach the popular Choke Creek Falls.
5.60	9.02	Bear left and cross a side channel of Butler Run; questionable water quality. More good camping in this area. Next, the trail walks alongside the main run; acceptable water quality.
5.79	9.32	Turn right and cross some planks that are all that remain from an archaic wooden bridge over Butler Run that washed away sometime in recent years. Then turn left and continue downstream.
5.83	9.39	After a broad curve to the right, the trail is now following Choke Creek upstream.
5.98	9.63	Reach Choke Creek Falls, featuring a drop of about eleven feet into a pool, then another drop of about four feet into a second pool. The pools are great spots for swimming and there are many boulders for sitting down and taking a break. Next, the Pinchot Trail curves to the right and passes through a great campsite. Choke Creek Falls is one of the jewels of the Pocono region, and it can only be reached on foot. Many casual visitors reach this spot via an old forestry road

MI	KM	DESCRIPTION
(cont.)		that comes in from Phelps Road to the northeast. The managers of Pinchot State Forest prefer that visitors walk to this spot via the Pinchot Trail.
6.10	9.82	Hop over a small run (poor water quality) then pass a riffle in Choke Creek. Taking water from Choke Creek is not advised because it is a low-lying waterway that has collected many tributaries, and you will soon find that it has been dammed many times by beavers, which alters natural filtration processes.
6.36	10.25	Note the system of large open meadows to the left. The trail is trending away from Choke Creek.
6.58	10.60	Pass through a very rocky area then curve right alongside a small run, going upstream. Good camping in this area.
6.64	10.70	Turn left and cross the run; questionable water quality.
6.87	11.07	Reach Choke Creek again and turn right, upstream. More good camping around this turn.
6.94	11.17	Pass by a wide spot in the creek with lots of driftwood strewn all about. This is probably the site of several beaver dams that were recently wiped out by stormy weather. The trail then heads inland again.
7.02	11.30	Scramble up a minor ridgeline.
7.23	11.64	Reach Choke Creek yet again and turn right, upstream. In this area, the creek spreads out into several channels trickling through an extensive wetland.
7.30	11.75	Turn left, cross an unnamed run (poor water quality), then turn right alongside Choke Creek once more.
7.46	12.02	Turn sharply right and head inland.
7.52	12.11	Turn left at a trail junction. The yellow-blazed trail to the right is an old route of the Pinchot Trail. When the Pinchot Trail was rerouted to Choke Creek Falls in 2018, the old route became known as the

The scenic Choke Creek, upstream from the falls.

MI	KM	DESCRIPTION
(cont.)		Choke Creek Nature Trail, which eventually leads north to Tannery Road and can be used to form loop hikes.
7.56	12.18	Great campsite. The trail curves right and follows a side channel of the creek up to a swampy area that is popular with beavers.
7.74	12.46	Turn right alongside Choke Creek again.
7.94	12.78	Turn right under an enormous old hemlock. Follow a side channel of the creek briefly then rise to higher ground.
7.99	12.87	Pass to the right of an excellent camping area under tall pines, then head back to the creekside.
8.28	13.33	Turn right for a brief detour inland, before heading back to the creekside.
8.75	14.09	Reach an extensive beaver dam complex (as of 2024), forming a sizeable pond at a spot where the creek previously made a sharp turn in a meadow.

A complex of beaver dams on Choke Creek.

MI	KM	DESCRIPTION
8.79	14.15	The Pinchot Trail departs from Choke Creek for the final time. Turn right and briefly follow a small tributary run upstream (questionable water quality).
8.82	14.20	Turn right again and begin a moderate climb.
9.12	14.68	The trail has leveled off on top of the plateau above the Choke Creek watershed.
9.33	15.02	The trail bears left onto an old road or railroad grade that heads in a relatively straight line to the northeast, though it is heavily overgrown with mountain laurel and giant rhododendron. It is also excessively muddy.
9.55	15.37	Turn right at a double blaze, where the trail tries to avoid an even muddier area. Here the trail builders added some lengthy meanders as a scenic route through a pretty area of hemlocks, white pines, and mountain laurel, followed by mature high-altitude woods.
9.82	15.82	Cross a small run on rocks; poor water quality.

MI	KM	DESCRIPTION
10.47	16.86	Keep right at a nice but dry campsite under hemlocks.
10.51	16.92	Turn right and rejoin the old grade that marches to the northeast. Proceed through a very dense jungle of giant rhododendron.
10.65	17.15	Turn left at a trail junction, on to a new segment of the Pinchot Trail that was built in 2018 to eliminate a lengthy walk on Tannery Road. The former route goes straight ahead and is now blazed yellow. That trail leads 0.24 mi (0.38 km) in a straight line to a parking area on Tannery Road. After turning left at the junction, the modern Pinchot Trail pokes through an excessively rocky zone, then rambles rather easily across the flat landscape. There are some more rocky zones and muddy spots along the way though.
11.30	18.19	Bear right briefly on a double-dirt-track logging road then turn left back into the woods. As of 2024, rocks around the two junctions have been painted pink by someone alerting hikers to this turn. It works.
11.65	18.77	Turn left onto a grassy lane that runs parallel to a deer fence (as of 2024). This type of fence is used by foresters to keep deer out of an area where the forest is regenerating, because deer eat young tree saplings as soon as they emerge from the ground. Smaller animals can pass through the fence, and occasional gates allow access for hunters. Areas with too many deer have few new trees and the existing trees grow old and die with no replacements. This is a serious problem for forest health throughout Pennsylvania.
11.78	18.97	Go straight ahead where the grassy lane and deer fence turn right (as of 2024).
11.83	19.05	Turn right and briefly encounter an upper tributary of Choke Creek; acceptable water quality. Good camping in this area, though the ground is quite rocky. Choke Creek itself is off in the distance to the left.

MI	KM	DESCRIPTION
11.93	19.21	Hop across a muddy and surprisingly deep stream; questionable water quality.
12.00	19.32	At the edge of a large meadow, turn sharply right (north).
12.11	19.51	The trail is marching in a mostly straight line directly to the north, hugging the boundary between Pinchot State Forest (right) and State Game Lands #91 (left). For a while, Tannery Road is visible through the trees to the right.
12.40	19.96	Hop across another small upper tributary of Choke Creek (acceptable water quality) and immediately bear left. The trail then straightens out and resumes its march to the north. Avoid the private land just to the left of the trail. There are some challenging muddy spots in this area.
12.86	20.71	Turn right briefly on Bear Lake Road, at a sign for the Behler Swamp Trail. After crossing the culvert over a small run, the Pinchot Trail crosses the road and continues northbound on the former White Line Trail. (If you are hiking the South Section only, walk east on Bear Lake Road for 0.43 mi [0.69 km] to the parking lot at the corner of Tannery Road.)

NORTH SECTION

MI	KM	DESCRIPTION
12.86	20.71	The Pinchot Trail crosses Bear Lake Road right next to the county line and joins the former White Line Trail, heading to the north. (If you are completing the North Section only, you will have reached this point after walking west on the road; in that case turn right at the signpost.)
13.08	21.07	Turn left on a logging road to avoid a private property boundary.
13.12	21.12	Where the logging road turns left, continue straight ahead on a footpath, still with the private property boundary on your right.
13.18	21.23	Turn left on what appears to be an old pipeline swath.
13.25	21.33	Cross the logging road again, then just a few yards later, watch carefully for an abrupt right turn off the pipeline and onto trail. The Pinchot Trail now heads in a nearly straight line to the north, following the boundary between Pinchot State Forest (right) and private land (left). The logging road is just to your right for a while.
13.92	22.42	Pass a junction with the yellow-blazed Frank Gantz Trail. (That trail leads east about one mile and ends at the Pine Hill Trail, which in turn has junctions with the main Pinchot Trail to the north and south.)
14.07	22.65	The Pinchot Trail curves to the northeast to get around a low, swampy area.
14.37	23.14	Go over a boardwalk through a wet area. Next, climb up a minor ridgeline. The trail then resumes its steady march directly to the north.
14.51	23.36	Turn right on to a wide grassy lane. Follow this lane for the next 0.21 mi (0.35 km).

MI	KM	DESCRIPTION
14.57	23.45	Pass the junction with another grassy lane marked as the County Line Trail. The Pinchot Trail continues ahead and joins the pre-existing Pine Hill Trail.
14.72	23.71	Watch carefully for an abrupt left turn off the grassy lane and into the woods. The Pinchot Trail joins the former Scrub Oak Trail and heads north. Begin a long and very gradual descent. (The Pine Hill Trail continues on the grassy lane to the northeast, then eventually turns to the south to join the main Pinchot Trail again. Along the way, the Pine Hill Trail passes an intersection with a woods road that goes to a great vista, and it also intersects the Frank Gantz Trail. All of these features can be seen in the public use map for Pinchot State Forest.)
15.53	25.00	Pass through a rocky dip in the landscape. Next, the trail rises briefly then levels off for a while. There is a large logging zone just uphill to the left.
15.70	25.28	Cross Pittston Road and pass a sign for the Painter Creek Trail. (Just to the right, there are a couple of possible parking spots on the road.)
15.82	25.47	Cross an old woods road. Continue moderately downhill for the next 0.60 mi (0.97 km).
16.42	26.44	Curve right through a dark campsite under hemlocks, then cross Painter Creek. This will be a wet crossing during rainy periods. Of historical interest: "Painter" is an archaic Pennsylvania colloquialism for a panther or mountain lion. There is more good camping on the other side of the creek.
16.47	26.52	Pass a junction with the yellow-blazed Watres Trail. The Pinchot Trail begins a steep climb back out of the hollow. (The Watres Trail heads north into Painter Hollow before turning back south and traversing the plateautop and some wetlands to the east of the Pinchot Trail. It returns to the Pinchot Trail southeast of here.)

Painter Creek enters a bucolic campsite.

MI	KM	DESCRIPTION
16.60	26.73	Cross an unmarked trail that goes to some old campsites. The Pinchot Trail levels off for a while.
16.79	27.03	Climb steeply but briefly up a ridgeline.
16.83	27.10	Cross a recent (as of 2024) logging road, with active logging taking place in both directions. Note that the Pinchot Trail and a buffer zone have been preserved.
16.95	27.29	Turn abruptly right at a signpost denoting the Painter Creek Trail and Hays Run Trail. Proceed southbound across a gently rolling plateau-top landscape. Continue easily and uneventfully for the next 0.87 mi (1.40 km).
17.82	28.69	Turn left at a junction with the Spruce Hill Trail.
18.13	29.20	Climb up a minor ridgeline amidst a pile of boulders. After the climb, note the wildflower-filled meadow on the right.
18.28	29.43	Another steep but relatively brief climb up a ridgeline.

MI	KM	DESCRIPTION
18.45	29.72	Near a signpost denoting the older North Line Trail, curve sharply to the right (south).
18.64	30.02	Pass your second encounter with the yellow-blazed Watres Trail. Note the large swamp on the left, which is populated by loudmouthed bullfrogs. After a few more curves, the trail proceeds in a nearly straight line to the south.
19.24	30.99	Walk around a vehicle gate and cross Sassafras Hill Road. There is a parking spot right next to this crossing. The Pinchot Trail joins the former Sassafras Hill Trail; curve to the right just after the road crossing.
19.72	31.76	Turn right and resume the southbound march you were on previously.
19.94	32.11	Turn sharply right (west). Next, the landscape becomes more variable and the trail dips into and climbs out of several low rocky areas.
20.42	32.89	Reach a scenic spot where the wide Spring Run emerges dramatically from under a large tree after some distance flowing underground. Good water quality, especially near the discharge point.
20.47	32.97	Turn left on Pittston Road (your second encounter with this road) and follow it south to the next trail junction.
20.54	33.08	Across from a parking area that serves several different trails, turn right off Pittston Road and onto the former Powder Magazine Trail. Begin a moderate climb back to the top of the plateau. Once on top, the Pinchot Trail meanders lazily through open woods. (Back on Pittston Road, do not turn onto the Bear Swamp Trail, which is a gated grassy lane.)
21.00	33.82	Cross a small run; questionable water quality.
21.14	34.04	Pass a junction with the yellow-blazed Pine Hill Trail.
21.22	34.17	Curve sharply to the left (south).

Spring Run re-emerges after flowing underground.

MI	KM	DESCRIPTION
21.49	34.60	Reach the largest trail register box this longtime hiker has ever seen. Please sign in.
21.56	34.71	Reach a large state forest parking area and head down the driveway. This is a convenient parking spot if you are doing the North Section or the entire Pinchot Trail System, though it is not directly situated on the South Section.
21.61	34.79	Turn right (west) on Bear Lake Road and follow it for the next 0.61 mi (0.98 km).
22.21	35.77	Reach the parking lot at the corner of Bear Lake Road and Tannery Road. This is the end of the Pinchot Trail System as described in this guide; the loop begins again by turning left into the trees behind the lot.

Pinchot Trail System (North Section)

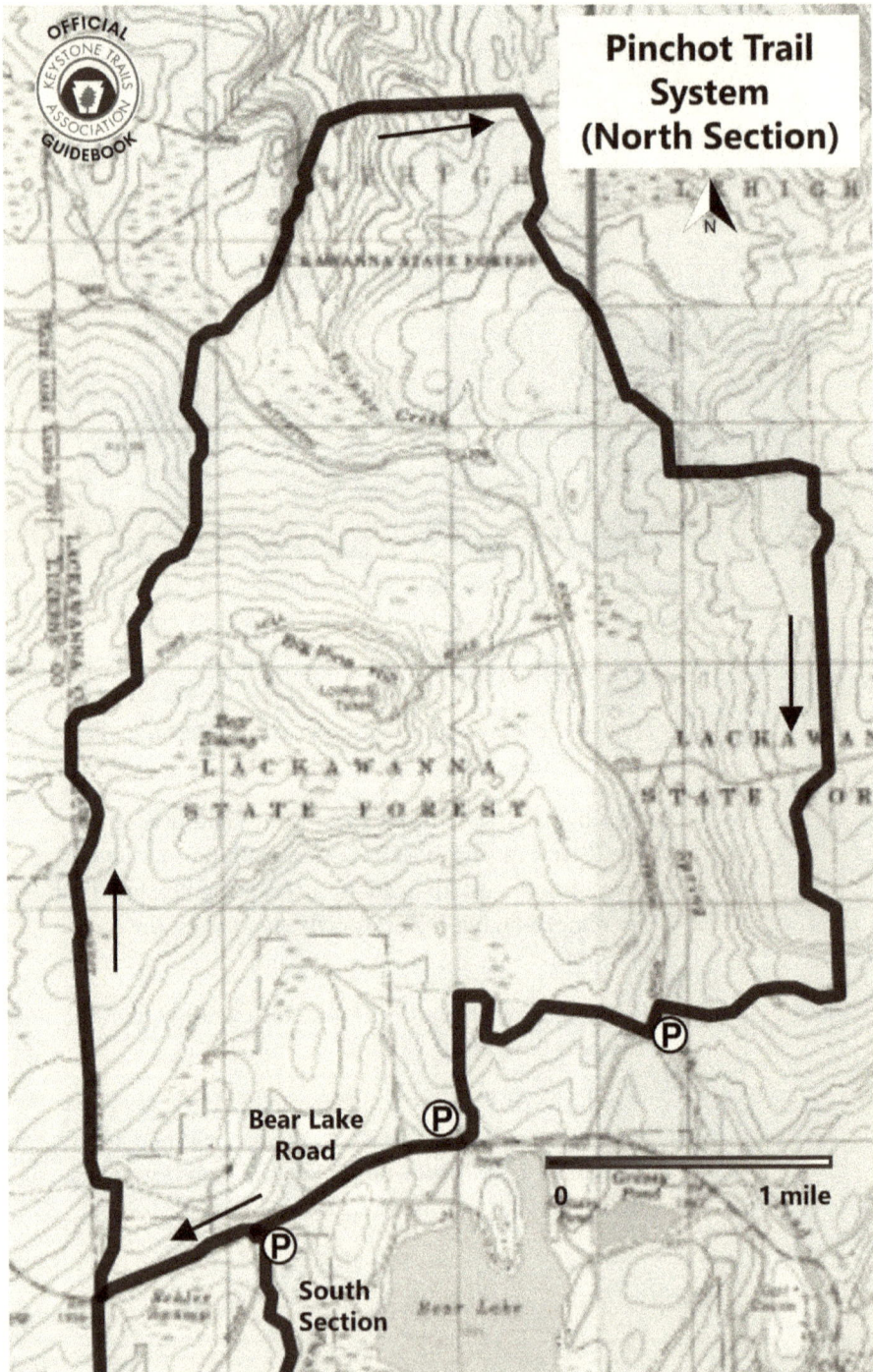

North
Section

Bear Lake
Road

**Pinchot Trail System
(South Section)**

N

L E H I G H

Ⓟ Tannery
Road

L A C K A W A
S T A T E   F O

L A C K A W A N N A
S T A T E   F O R E S T

Choke Creek
Falls

OFFICIAL
KEYSTONE TRAILS
ASSOCIATION
GUIDEBOOK

0   1 mile

For a larger online map of the Pinchot Trail System,
visit Keystone Trails Association at:

www.kta-hike.org/maps

or scan here:

Note: "Lackawanna State Forest" as shown in the map backgrounds on
the previous two pages is now known as Pinchot State Forest.

These maps illustrate GPS data collected by the author. The online map
is courtesy of CalTopo. The printed map on the previous two pages was
created with GPS Visualizer, founded and operated by Adam Schneider,
with USGS (United States Geologic Survey) maps as the backgrounds.
All maps and data are verified for accuracy by the author and Keystone
Trails Association.

ABOUT THE AUTHOR

Ben Cramer has hiked more than 6,000 miles on Pennsylvania's hiking trails and has completed many of the state's long-distance backpacking trails multiple times. He is a longtime member of Keystone Trails Association and was a member of its board of directors from 2018 to 2023. He is also a member of several Pennsylvania conservation groups and hiking clubs, and he was formerly an executive committee member for Sierra Club at both the local and state levels.

Cramer is the author of seven guidebooks for Pennsylvania backpacking trails, including one previous edition for the Thunder Swamp Trail. With one exception, none of those long-distance trails had dedicated guidebooks previously. Cramer was also the editor of *Pennsylvania Hiking Trails* (13th edition, 2008). For several years he wrote regularly on outdoor adventure and environmental issues for *The Centre Daily Times* and for a variety of Pennsylvania volunteer publications.

Under his professional name Benjamin W. Cramer, he is the author of the book *Freedom of Environmental Information* (2011). He is a longtime resident of State College, PA and teaches for the Donald P. Bellisario College of Communications at Penn State University, where one of his research specialties is the environmental impacts of modern telecommunications services.

www.ingramcontent.com/pod-product-compliance
Lightning Source LLC
Chambersburg PA
CBHW022348040426
42449CB00006B/771